WHAT COMES FIRST?

Rob Olliges

Rourke

Publishing LLC

Vero Beach, Florida 32964

www.rourkepublishing.com

PHOTO CREDITS: All Photo's © 2007 Renee Brady

Editor: Robert Stengard-Olliges

Cover design by Nicola Stratford.

Library of Congress Cataloging-in-Publication Data

What comes first?
 p. cm. -- (My first math)
 ISBN 1-59515-977-0 (Hardcover)
 ISBN 1-59515-948-7 (Paperback)
 1. Sequences (Mathematics)--Juvenile literature. 2. Printing presses--Juvenile literature. 3. Picture books--Juvenile literature.
I. Title.
 QA292.G73 2007
 686--dc22
                          2006019794

Printed in the USA

CG/CG

Rourke Publishing

www.rourkepublishing.com – sales@rourkepublishing.com
Post Office Box 3328, Vero Beach, FL 32964

01 09

Table of Contents

Get Ready

Today I get to bake my first cake. My Mom will help me, but what comes first?

It takes many steps to make a cake. Mom helps me from the first step to the last step.

A **recipe** tells me everything I need and shows me the steps to make a cake. Mom and I read the recipe together.

We have everything we need to make a cake. What comes next?

Mix the Batter

Next we **preheat** the oven so it will be hot when we need it. While the oven warms up, Mom and I mix the butter, sugar, eggs, **flour**, milk, baking powder, and a little salt.

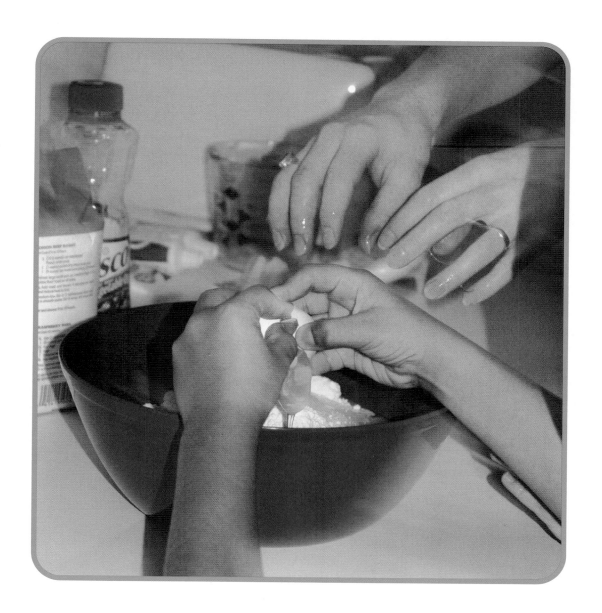

I mix the **ingredients** together and they become cake **batter**. Stirring is hard so Mom helps me. We stir the batter until it is smooth.

When all the batter is **smooth**, we pour it in cake pans. Now what comes next?

Bake the Cake

Next we put the pans into the hot oven, shut the door, and set the **timer**. Fifty minutes and don't open the door. What happens next?

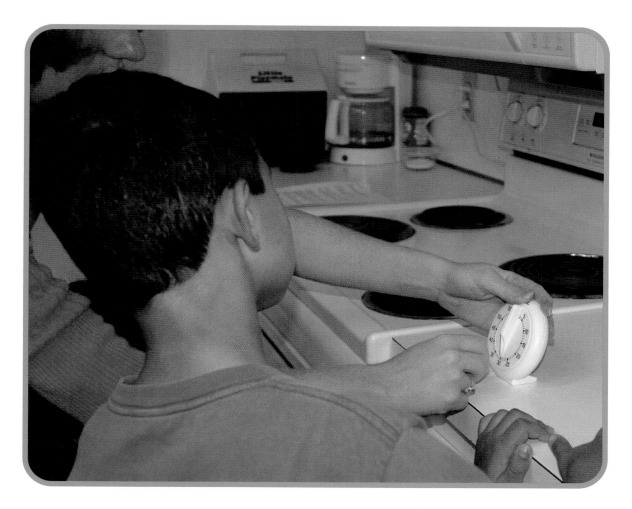

Now the hot oven cooks the batter. The batter changes in the heat. Mom tells me that the baking powder helps change the batter into cake.

The timer RINGS and we peek in the oven. It looks like a cake now. It is taller than before and not gooey like batter. Mom has a trick to see if the cake is ready.

Toothpick

Mom lets me put a **toothpick** in the cake. If it comes out clean, the cake is done baking.

Clean Up

The cake is very hot and has to cool off. Now it is time to clean up our mess. We wash the bowls and spoons and clean up the kitchen. When we are done, the cake should be cool.

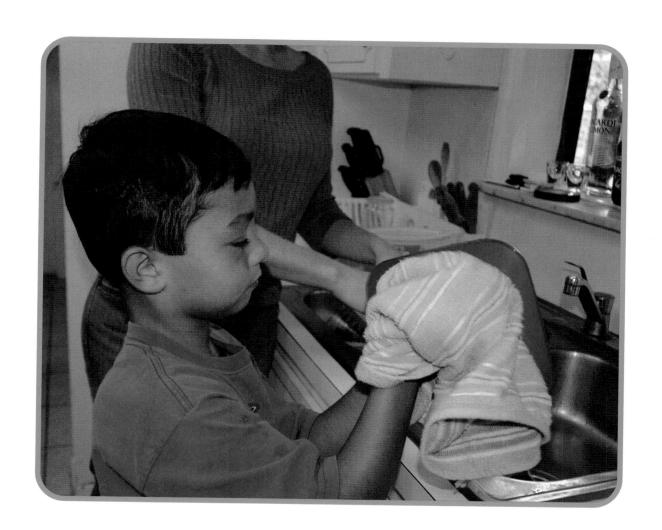

Decorate the Cake

Now the cake is cool and the kitchen is clean. It is time to **decorate** the cake. The colors we like are white, purple, and yellow.

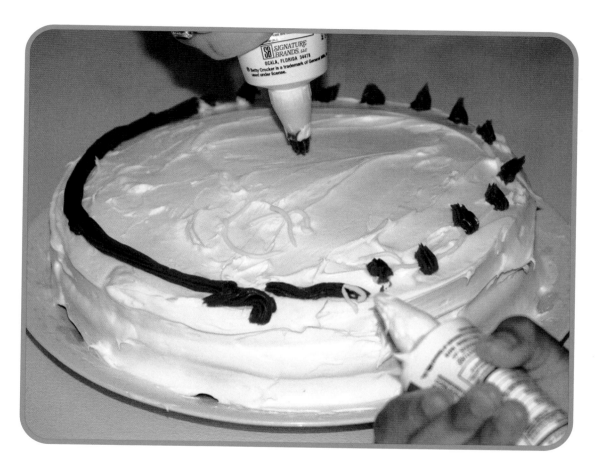

Almost done!

We have mixed the batter, baked the cake, cleaned the kitchen, and decorated the cake. Mom has helped from the first step to the last.

Now what comes next?

Now we can eat the cake. This is the best day of my life!

Glossary

batter (BAT ur)- a mixture of milk, eggs, and flour used to make cakes

decorate (DEK uh rate)- adding things to make something prettier

flour (FLOU ur)- ground wheat used for baking

ingredient (in GREE dee uhnt)- one of the items that something is made of

preheat (pri HEET)- to warm up before cooking

recipe (RESS I pee)- instructions for preparing and cooking food

smooth (smooTH)- a surface that is even and flat, not rough or bumpy

timer (TIME ur)- a device that lets you know when a certain time is up

toothpick (TOOTH pik)- a small, thin piece of wood or plastic used to remove food from between the teeth

Index

Further Reading

Bastyra, J. *Cooking*. Creative Company, 2004.
Lewis, Sara. *Kids' Baking : 60 Delicious Recipes for Children to Make*. Sterling, 2006.
Taylor-Butler, Christine. *Step-by-Step*. Children's Press, 2005.

Websites To Visit

www.homebaking.org
www.bettycrocker.com/baking/kidss/kids_friendly_baking.aspx
www.howthecookiecrumbles.com

About The Author

Rob Olliges grew up baking with his grandmothers and enjoys watching his kids bake with their grandmothers. He also enjoys writing children's books and eating cake.